The Nostalgic Sun

Elise Ryskamp

Thank you…

to all the artists that have inspired me with their courage and art.

to the friends that motivated and helped me along the way.

to my editor and dear friend for sticking with me through life.

and to my family for fostering creativity at a young age and supporting me in my endeavors.

i told myself it didn't mean anything.

but it did.

the way you made me feel worthy
like no one ever has

it meant something.

April 25 2015 9:03pm

Elise Ryskamp

I'm not fine
I'm not okay
I'm not myself
I'm lost in my being
drowning in my soul
fading into all my thoughts

I don't know how I got here

all I know is that my song is on
and I can't remember the words
I can't taste my food
I'm speaking but the words aren't mine
the fire is burning me but I can't feel it

for my brain is not of my body

October 12 2015 11:12pm

you see a body but i am a soul

July 14 2016 10:14pm

the sun had set on the past
and had risen in the future
much brighter than before
yet I still yearned
for the dull sun

    -nostalgia

        August 3 2016 10:37pm

There are some places in this world that just stick with us.

For me it is this old rickety dock. The sounds that flood the dock at night are eerie yet calming. The charming laughter and purring motors of the day have ceased. And been replaced with silence among the lapping water, hopeful of the next day's adventure.

However, there is so much unknown that lies between the adventure and hope. So much cold and murky water. Yet that's what makes the water intriguing, that's what makes the unknown so tempting.

August 28 2016 10:48pm

what if our nightmares are disguised as day dreams
…
because for me the bad is the good times I had with
you.

the heat of spring that was beating on and between us
the buzzing bees that were silenced
by the way you looked at me

for me the bad is the first time you called me beautiful
because I knew what you meant,
that the way I leaned into you was beautiful
that the way my body touched yours was beautiful

all the times that you opened the door for me
you were just hoping the favor would be returned.
all your goodbye kisses
I should have known they weren't filled with nectar

for me the bad is the good times
because this time
I know that a bee will sting
just for some honey

September 21 2016 9:06pm

The Nostalgic Sun

how is it
that the same name that lit up my face
lit up my phone screen
lit a fire in my eyes
can now make my smile fall off my face in seconds?

that same face
still makes me heart race
but not for the same reason
that it used to

September 21 2016 9:09pm

Elise Ryskamp

long football nights
chanting under the shining lights
the smell of bonfire smoke
all these remind me of the hearts that broke
two years back in September
no matter how hard I try not to, I still remember
just how I let you go
never wanted to though
then I never knew what to say
when I would pass you in the hallway
seeing someone that couldn't be mine
unsure about His design
now I understand his way
but to this day
when I look in your eyes
I still see the sparks fly

October 19 2016 9:39pm

I love that I can hear my father's sneezes from all the way downstairs. I love that I can smell my mother's cooking from my bedroom. I can hear the pounding of a hammer on a nail putting together the newest home improvement project. And I can hear the news that my mother watches while making dinner. I love that I can hear my father's obnoxious mannerisms that drive my mother crazy. I love seeing the scattered piles of my mother's craft supplies that drive my father crazy. I love the tools that are strayed throughout the house that my father uses to somehow fix anything. I love all the lists and sticky notes that my mother somehow manages our family with.

I love the simplistic days where we all sit in one room on the same piece of furniture even though we have so many that we could be spread out on.

This is what makes a house a home.

January 7 2017 10:39pm

Elise Ryskamp

my mother asked what happened with you.
            I said I didn't know…
she said you seemed nice.
            I said "he did
                    didn't he…"
she asked if I still see you around
            I said I haven't seen *you*
                    for a while…
she said some people are like flowers
            bringing seasonal joy
 but you weren't a flower
            you just wanted mine.

                    March 20 2017 1:00pm

I'm shedding you
little by little
memory by memory
but I wish I could shed
the entire coat
all at once
for a fresh body
-just like the serpent
you said I was.

March 28 2017 1:00pm

Elise Ryskamp

I never knew how much
words could sting
until I sat in that chair
and heard you say
the words that I couldn't
the words that I hadn't been able to say
nor comprehend
the words
rang in my ears
like church bells on repeat
you kept talking but all
that I could hear was that
I still wasn't good enough

March 28 2017 11:09pm

she says she wishes
she knew me better
but if she really knew
who I was she wouldn't
want to know me
at all

March 28 2017 11:10pm

slow motion
eyes scanning the words
searching for the news
I had been waiting for
and when I found it
the ink seemed to pulse
like my heart in my chest
that dropped to the floor
along with the letter
and all of the Hope that I had left

March 28 2017 11:12pm

you only recognized me
in the dark
-that should've been
my first clue
you fed me lies
because I was your prey
I said no but you
weren't expecting an answer
hearing my name in your mouth
disgusted me
I untangled my feet from your trap
as my bare feet ran along
the water I understood
the reality.

-do you always get what you want?

April 10 2017 1:07pm

she'll laugh at your jokes when no one else does
she'll remember all the little things about you
she'll heal the broken places in your heart
she'll find the positivity in the negativity
she'll care more than she should
she'll see the best in you even when you treat her
poorly
she'll hold your hand when your crying
she'll go to the ends of the earth to make you happy
she'll tell you that you look good no matter how many
times you ask
she'll believe in you when you don't believe in
yourself
she'll come over and make you get out of bed and get
dressed when you are moping
she'll listen to you no matter how much you have to
say
she'll walk through the dark days with you
she'll be happy for you even when she is disappointed
she'll cheer you on and will be the loudest in the
crowd
she'll turn the most boring day into the most exciting
day
she'll hold you accountable
she'll bring over your favorite comfort foods when
you need a night in
she'll make you feel valued
she'll remind you why life is worth living
she'll put your needs above hers
she'll randomly call just to talk
she'll make your dreams her dreams
she'll make you laugh so hard your stomach hurts

she'll make you laugh when laughing is the last thing
you want to do
she'll always have your back and look out for you
she'll care for you even on *her* worst days
she'll stand by you during your mistakes
she'll tell you what you may not want to hear but need
to hear
she'll surprise you and spoil you
she'll remind you of who you are when you forget
      and most of all
     she'll love you with her whole heart.
        -a best friend

April 10 2017 11:01pm

Elise Ryskamp

I used to think there was beauty in pain
but now I see the truth-
the world tries to beautify brokenness
to mask the harsh reality,
        --it's a bloody hell of suffering
tell me how can suffering ever be beautiful?

April 11 2017 12:49pm

people see her money
and wish they could have it
and she says take it
take it so you can see
why they call it

    filthy rich.

      April 16 2017 10:06pm

Elise Ryskamp

we drink
to silence our thoughts
only to wake up
with new lingering voices
we smoke
to feel at peace
with ourselves
only to find
that the high makes reality harder
we sleep together
to feel something
anything at all-
and leave in the morning
more broken than before
we chase moments
not solutions.

but what are the
solutions then?

May 1 2017 12:30pm

you don't have to hear the words
to know what they said

May 3 2017 12:30pm

Elise Ryskamp

the other day you asked me
how soccer was going
i haven't played soccer
since i was 8.

it's been 10 years since you've asked me about myself.

May 7 2017 2:00pm

sometimes i wonder how you are

and then the halls tell me you are doing just fine.

May 7 2017 12:30pm

Elise Ryskamp

I'm worshipping with clenched fists
but at least I'm worshipping, right?

May 22 2017 9:28pm

the world revolves around the sun
the moon revolves around the world
even the universe is a love triangle

May 22 2017 9:28pm

Elise Ryskamp

you are content
with just talking
        actually just talking.
you are the first
to want to know
the ins and outs of me
in a way that is different
from any of the others

            May 22 2017 10:15pm

when a heart breaks
it may heal
but it never returns to the way it was before
it beats differently
        stronger in some areas
                and weaker in others

June 1 2017 6:24pm

i hate missing you
when i miss you, I'm missing a part of myself
because you remind me of who i am
…
i miss myself

June 2 2017 1:01pm

she talked to him for the first time in a while
the wound had healed and she felt strong enough
when they saw each other, there was no hatred in their
eyes
no suffering, no distant 'how could you'
it was a simple fragile hello
it was a hello to a new start
without forgetting the old ending
his smile was still the same
the smile that she fell for
and then the smile that broke her
but now it had a more complex meaning
it was just an old smile
that reminded her of her past
what had been and what had become
his smile captured the last 4 years
and looking at it now felt like watching a movie
you've seen a thousand times
but yet each time it brings you something different

July 5 2017 9:56pm

dream big
but not too big
be successful
but not too successful
be strong
but not too strong
be skinny
but not too skinny
be emotional
but not too emotional
be wealthy
but not too wealthy
be modest
but not too modest
be bold
but not too bold
be loud
but not too loud
be spontaneous
but not too spontaneous
be fun
but not too fun
be smart
but not too smart
be hardworking
but not too hardworking
be passionate
but not too passionate

-but why can't I just be me?

July 5 2017 10:02pm

my shoulders ache
from looking over them
with my eyes that burn with fear
pepper spray escorts me everywhere
for my feet can only run so fast
the night is my prison
and the day is my jail

    -womenity

            July 5 2017 10:38pm

Elise Ryskamp

it's not that i'm ungrateful
but that i do not need
all that i have

    July 13 2017 2:36pm

while you were sitting in the terminal
I was taking the stage for the last time
while you were boarding the plane
I was blowing out my candles on my 18th birthday
while you were preparing for take off
I was going home to an abandoned house
while you were sleeping up in the clouds
I was wide awake under them

    -on March 2nd

        July 13 2017 2:53pm

Elise Ryskamp

sometimes what you admire the most about others
is actually their biggest insecurity

July 13 2017 5:16pm

growing up
I use to wake up in the middle of the night
because I couldn't sleep
for my legs hurt
my mother said it was growing pains
and now
I still wake up in the middle of the night
because I can't sleep
for my heart hurts
from the growing pains…

July 16 2017 10:55PM

you were a hurricane
that flooded my mind
and conquered my heart

July 20 2017 7:08pm

it was all so fast
my mind was drowning in your hands
and even when we came up for breath
my mind was still swimming
in and out of the moment
swaying between the wants of my body and heart

-i just..

July 23 2017 11:20pm

Elise Ryskamp

for once i have found someone
who doesn't steal my breath from me
but reminds me to breathe easily

July 25 2017 5:42pm

you never stayed in one place for too long
but I stayed here
wondering…
all summer long
and now that it is ending
I wonder….
do you miss me?
or was I just another state
that you were passing through?

August 6 2017 11:31pm

Elise Ryskamp

we never started
but i think we ended

August 6 2017 11:31pm

today is August 6
you came home today
but I wasn't at the airport

today is the day
I've been waiting for
but now it's just another day

and you're just another guy
another memory
another time

and I think that's what hurts the most
I really didn't think that's all you were
I really didn't think that's all we were
but that's all for now

August 6 2017 11:34pm

Elise Ryskamp

they'll tell you
how to get over
the liar
the cheater
the player
but no one tells you
how to get over
the one that treated you right
       and I'm starting to wonder
       if it's because

       no one knows how.

            August 8 2017 11:34pm

my hands are naked
and my toes are cold
without yours wrapped around them

seeing your name
at the top of my screen
and knowing that's the closest
that you can ever be to me

August 14 2017 7:20pm

Elise Ryskamp

one day i felt everything with you
and the next i felt it all fall
and then i felt nothing at all

- "moving on"

August 14 2017 7:20pm

all we ever want to know is that they miss us too
because we want to know we gave them something
worthy of missing
that *we* are worthy of missing
but in reality
at some point, we must walk away
with or without an answer
and accept that their love does not define us.

and that my friends is the hardest lesson to
learn of all.

August 21 2017 12:37 am

Elise Ryskamp

we created our own space
we were space

August 28 2017 11:45pm

it was as though I could see the sparks between our
fingers
 as our skin grazed each other's
it was as if I could see the blur of the world spinning
around us
and the stars revolving around our hearts
as we talked about everything under the sun
I could feel all of our planets align
I could feel gravity lose its grip on my being
'cause we were the galaxy
never-ending and to be discovered

      -traverse

           August 28 2017 11:55pm

my father used to ask me
what I tell people
when they ask "what are your parents like?"
I avoided answering him when he asked
because I could not find the words
to capture all that there is to know
I did not know how to explain that
my father
is the most hardworking and dedicated man that I have
ever met
is one of the best examples of willpower
is the biggest kid at heart
my mother
is the most selfless person I have ever met
is one of the most beautiful thinkers
is full of passion

my father used to ask me
what I tell people
when they ask "where did you learn that?"
I told him that I say
it was just how I was raised
because it was less words than saying
my father
taught me to be independent
taught me to have determination to keep going
taught me not to take life so seriously
and
my mother
taught me to think, create, dream, and wonder
taught me to be who I am and love who I am
taught me to have a loving spirit for everyone

so when people ask me
how I got to where I am today
how I became who I am today
I will say

my father and my mother.

August 29 2017 11:31pm

Elise Ryskamp

my soul will forever be searching for yours
in everyone i meet

September 1 2017 7:08pm

your touch is a flame
igniting my heart
and burning it at the same time

September 13 2017 10:13pm

Elise Ryskamp

I called you that night
but you weren't on the other line
I searched for you everywhere
in everyone
but you weren't there

it was your voicemail
that awakened my reality
-you were a world away
and these people
were nothing but strangers

-you are more than *just a phone call away*

September 22 2017 4:00pm

you will always be there for me but you can't always
be *here* for me.

September 22 2017 4:00pm

Elise Ryskamp

searching for happiness
at the bottom of a bottle

-funny how at the end
of the night
the bottles are always broken.

September 28 2017 11:25pm

my words
when I was speechless
my brain
was I was thoughtless
my backbone
when I was spineless
my heart
when I was heartless
my eyes
when I was sightless

-you made me more when I was less

October 5 2017 2:12pm

Elise Ryskamp

when the storm comes
and you find yourself cursing the skies
just remember
you were not born strong
you were made strong

October 5 2017 10:15pm

you asked me
     why I was so afraid to love?
to which I answered
     what is your most prized possession?
     what is it that you worked relentlessly on,
         poured blood sweat and tears into?

          Is it your 1st place trophies
          that are locked in their cage?
          or is it the car in your driveway
          that you never let anyone else
          drive?

because mine is my heart
     and just like you
I fear that someone will destroy it.

          October 5 2017 11:40pm

Elise Ryskamp

I am like the ocean tide
I am high
and then I am low
but all I want
is to lie on the beach

October 6 2017 12:02am

I am like the moon in the sky

I am near
and then I am far

and when I am far
the water misses me
and when I am near
the water kisses the land

we sway but we are never
one with each other

October 6 2017 12:02am

Elise Ryskamp

my dear I hope and pray
that you never have to get over
the sweet boy
I hope you never know what it's like
to lose him
I hope you get to call him yours forever
because he will be the hardest one
to let go of...

October 16 2017 11:34pm

sometimes when I put our playlist on
and drive around town
I can still hear you singing along
and I fear the day that I can't
hear that voice anymore

October 20 2017 10:14pm

Elise Ryskamp

i am missing my heart
and i don't even know who has it anymore

October 21 2017 10:25 am

we were reckless
playing with fire
throwing it around
like it was nothing
breathing in the smoke
thinking it would get us to cloud nine
never stopping to think
how much it could kill

-love

October 21 10:25am

Elise Ryskamp

when i come home
i leave my shoes at the door
and hang up my smile

October 27 2017 4:27pm

as a little girl
I dreamed
of all the places I would go
of all the things I would do

but never did I dream
of being here
with these shackles around my ankles
and this number on my chest

Oct 27 2017 4:21pm

Elise Ryskamp

but my dear
in order to get to where you are going
you must pass through forests of darkness
and mountains of snow
because it is then
that the stars will find you
and guide you to where you are supposed to be

Oct 27 2017 4:33pm

every night when i turn out the lights
i think of you

the dark has a way of bringing out my demons

November 3 2017 1:30pm

I was supposed to be happy
to finally be happy

but now I take pills to dull the pain
of how much it hurts
to have to wake up
to this nightmare everyday

-prescription for reality

November 27 2017 3:19pm

i wish nightmares remained in the night

November 27 2017 3:19pm

Elise Ryskamp

I grew up picking flowers in the fields
and bringing them in to decorate the dinner table
listening to the sweet country music
with my father
under the hood of my little blue pickup truck
I grew up with the smell of
a fire burning
and an engine running
always working as hard as I played

and no matter how far I go
never will I forget where I came from

November 28 2017 11:31pm

you are the monster under my bed

December 1 2017 12:00am

I'm not mad at you for hurting me

I'm mad at you for hurting who i was

December 1 2017 12:03am

my world shattered on the pavement that night.

and when I stood up I saw strangers
standing on the edge of my darkness
watching.
…
my world shattered

and this time there was no one there
to help remove the glass from my skin
so that I could pick up the pieces

December 4 2017 9:13pm

Elise Ryskamp

we swore that we wouldn't miss this place
we swore that we would be okay
but we were just kids
      who thought they were adults
because we knew everything about *our* world
and nothing about the real world

we didn't know that
this was the freest that we would ever be
that the country roads engrained on the backs of our
hands
were not limitations
but were maps guiding us to where we needed to be
and who we needed to become

                December 6 2017 1:50pm

just because the distance is gone
does not change the fact
that our souls are worlds apart

December 22 2017 10:34pm

i miss who you were

the world needed who you were.

January 7 2018 7:30pm

i have lost the keys to my own heart

January 21 2018 9:03pm

Elise Ryskamp

it was moving day
so i packed up my pain
and put it in boxes
to take home and unpack

May 17 2018 1:30pm

i find tears laying around
and wonder whose they are
not able to realize

    they're mine.

       May 28 2018 10:14pm

Elise Ryskamp

I let my boxes sit
in the back of my closet
for I was fearful
of what I would find inside of them

I danced around them for so long
I sugar coated them with denial
until one day I realized
that I could not remember

    what it felt like to dance freely

so I removed them from the shelf
and I began to unpack

    July 11 2018 7:08pm

don't be fooled…

healing feels a lot like breaking

July 18 2018 1:54pm

Elise Ryskamp

there is no love more beautiful
than the love for one's self.

July 19 2018 3:22pm

I pray that one day you can see

the poetry within your own story.

July 23 2018 10:05pm

Cover designed by Carolina Mogollón

Made in the USA
Lexington, KY
16 August 2018